Winter Vanquished
SPRING

An Anthology

Ian Field

Visit us online at www.authorsonline.co.uk

A Bright Pen Book

Copyright © Ian Field 2010
First published in Great Britain by Bright Pen 2010

Cover design © Roderick Field (*fieldafield.com*)

All rights reserved. No part of this publication may be reproduced, stored in a retrieval system, or transmitted in any form or by any means, electronic, mechanical, photocopy, recording or otherwise, without prior written permission of the copyright owner. Nor can it be circulated in any form of binding or cover other than that in which it is published and without similar condition including this condition being imposed on a subsequent purchaser.

British Library Cataloguing in Publication Data.
A catalogue record for this book is available from the British Library.

ISBN 978 0 7552 0634 6

Authors OnLine Ltd
19 The Cinques
Gamlingay, Sandy
Bedfordshire SG19 3NU
England

This book is also available in e-book format, details of which are available at www.authorsonline.co.uk

Despite our burdens or unchangeable histories we are, each and every one of us, capable of great exploits. We have the potential to make our own dreams become reality. I hope these words motivate, inspire and nurture that part of our being which we seem to neglect the most – the soul.

This anthology is a testimony to the invincible fortitude of the human spirit. I have seen it triumph over adversity, overcoming all obstacles to fulfil the purpose within. Life is difficult and it is easy to falter. May these poems stir you to action and awaken the courage to know that none of us stands alone.

Ian Field.

1st November 2010

Index

page

1. DAY OF RECKONING — 9
2. YOU ARE NOT ALONE — 11
3. NOW OR NEVER — 13
4. DEDICATION — 15
5. HIDDEN POTENTIAL — 17
6. GHOSTS OF CHRISTMAS PAST — 19
7. DON'T LOOK BACK IN ANGER — 21
8. PANDORA'S BOX — 23
9. WHERE ARE YOU NOW? — 25
10. SOMEWHERE OVER THE RAINBOW — 27
11. SEARCH FOR THE HERO INSIDE YOURSELF — 29
12. TOMORROW BELONGS TO ME — 31
13. KEEP YOUR EYES ON THE PRIZE — 33
14. PILGRIM'S PROGRESS — 35
15. GOLD MINING — 37
16. ONE MORE STEP ON THE ROAD TO JERUSALEM — 39
17. DREAM ON — 41
18. WHERE EAGLES SOAR — 43
19. NOW THANK WE ALL OUR GOD — 45
20. WHEN — 47
21. IF ONLY YOU BELIEVE — 49
22. REVIVAL FIRE — 51

page

23. GOD'S OWN PEOPLE	53
24. OBEDIENCE NOT SACRIFICE	55
25. FOR JERUSALEM'S SAKE	57
26. IT JUST AIN'T FUNNY	59
27. YOU CAN'T BRING ME DOWN	61
28. ROOTS	63
29. MAKING YOUR MIND UP	65
30. BE OF GOOD COURAGE	67
31. A LIGHT UNTO THE NATIONS	69
32. EYES THAT SEE	71
33. DELIGHT YOURSELF IN THE LORD	73
34. SPRINGS OF LIVING WATER	75
35. WE ARE MORE THAN CONQUERORS	77
36. THE LANGUAGE OF LOVE	79
37. GOD'S V.I.P.	81
38. TREASURE IN HEAVEN	83
39. MOVING TO HIGHER GROUND	85
40. DO THE RIGHT THING	87
41. RIVERS IN THE DESERT	89
42. HONOUR THE LORD	91
43. WAKE UP CALL	93

Winter Vanquished
SPRING

These poems are dedicated to

those who did not make it.

DAY OF RECKONING

I woke before the break of dawn,
My faith restored, my hope reborn.

I long to know of secrets deep,
To raise them from their slumbered sleep.

I heard God's voice addressed to me,
"The life you lead is blasphemy."

You have yet to have your finest hour,
A shining light, a bloom in flower.

Life is a matter of simple choices,
The silent scream of the dreaming voiceless.

It's time to act and take a stand,
To give, to lend a helping hand.

Just walk one day in broken shoes,
To empathise and pay your dues.

Within your soul a mustard seed,
It's immutable, a latent need.

Squandered gifts now dormant lie,
Don't close your eyes and walk on by.

Now turn your face into the light,
Meet destiny and do what's right.

YOU ARE NOT ALONE

I see your plight, I know your pain.
It's time to know of life again.
Desert days come to an end,
A light in darkness, a constant friend.

Return once more where you belong,
To fly, to soar, sing freedom's song.
Can you hear the church bells ringing?
Hope of hope and new life bringing.

Break the chains of dungeons deep,
Revived, refreshed by winter's sleep.
Seasons come and seasons go,
With mountains high and valleys low.

Prodigal son once wayward lost,
Your rubicon has now been crossed.
Vistas clear and pastures green,
Focus afresh on days unseen.

Trust in God to light the way,
To hear each prayer you daily pray.
Redeemed by grace to make amends,
For wasted lives and absent friends.

Justify the faith in you,
To do the best that you can do.
It's never too late to change your mind,
To choose to leave your past behind.

Live today with no regrets,
For time will heal what time forgets.
Each day you rise you're born again,
As sunshine always follows rain.

NOW OR NEVER

Take a look around you and tell me what you see,

A harvest of abundance or the fruits of a barren tree?

There is no explanation or mere alibi succinct,

Since cause and its effect are intrinsically linked.

Now nothing can be gained with scapegoats made to blame,

We are not all as innocent as we would like to claim.

So do not look at what you've lost nor grieve for what has gone,

Only look at what is left with which to carry on.

From the ashes of remembrance

A phoenix now can rise,

A seed brings forth new life

As yesterday's one dies.

Now is all we'll ever have, the present in our hands,

Not always as we wish it, according to our plans.

So seize the day with purpose

And let your beauty shine,

Blessed on high from God above

The glory will be thine.

DEDICATION

Lord, I dedicate my life to you,
I once believed, you always knew.
Hidden deep within my soul
I had a dream, a certain goal.

Nurtured through the mortal storm,
The darkest night, the promised dawn.
Snares and traps with pitfalls foil,
Blood and sweat plus tears of toil.

A fragile flicker ignites the flame,
A twist of fate to play the game.
Return once more to pastures new
Where fruit of the vine where one day grew.

Drifting through the perilous sea
The tempest calmed now shackles free.
Sheltered shore and solace found,
Captive's cry of homeward bound.

Turn again to heed the call,
Natural phase of rise and fall.
Love divine will always win,
Man of straw with heart of tin.

More precious than solid silver,
Still more coveted than gold.
With visions, signs and wonders
Your gift can't be bought or sold.

Time has come as rhymes can tell,
In love and war well all is well.
The past must die to live to dream,
Let hope excel your faith redeem.

HIDDEN POTENTIAL

It only takes one spark
To reignite the flame;
A light switch in the dark
To activate the chain.

A single word or action
Can turn the tide once more,
A simple first attraction,
The hope of what's in store.

A fleeting glimpse of freedom
The reason to aspire;
We find them when we need them
To escape the lifeless mire.

Misfortune's intervention
The struggle to survive,
Money's too tight to mention,
In the fight to stay alive.

When tested by the tempest
Or tempered by the fire,
The Sorcerer's Apprentice
Forever aiming higher.

Cast your net into the water,
Sowing seeds in fertile ground;
Place your gift upon the altar
And see the fruits of faith abound.

It is from tiny acorns planted
That mighty oaks will grow,
So take nothing now for granted
Just trust in all you know.

GHOSTS OF CHRISTMAS PAST

Standing at the graveside
With fresh flowers in your hand,
We still regret and can't forget
What we do not understand.

Where once you sent them roses
The brambles wildly grow,
Senses numb and tongues struck dumb
To let your feelings show.

The eulogies and epitaphs
Now echo in the past.
The memories may be fading
But the scars will always last.

A legacy of sorrow
With interest left to pay,
A blight upon tomorrow
Is the gift of yesterday.

Time may well be a healer
But some wounds do not heal,
As shadows cast by history
Can mould the way you feel.

The ripples in a mill pond
As the circles never end,
A myriad of obstacles
Why a broken heart won't mend.

Should old acquaintance be forgot
And never meet again,
A shooting star once dazzled
Now sadly on the wane.

DON'T LOOK BACK IN ANGER

Standing at the watershed
Past the point of no return,
With the wisdom of experience
We may live but never learn.

Reflections and reminders
In the mirror of your soul,
Lines etched by your encounters
As the years now take their toll.

Hindsight tinted spectacles
Can distort the bitter truth
As we boldly try to recall
The halcyon days of youth.

Of summers lost in reverie,
And never ending dream,
Mere tantalising glimpses
Of what we can't redeem.

But yesterday is over
And tomorrow never comes
As reality and fiction
Both dance to different drums.

No fanfares, bows or encores,
No triumphant curtain call;
Just echoes of a melody
As the teardrops start to fall.

Be thankful of small mercies,
We will always want for more;
But it's better to have loved and lost
Than be never loved before.

PANDORA'S BOX

Standing on the precipice
The race is all but run,
A classic case of crash and burn
Because you flew too near the sun.

Whilst skating close to danger
Yet blind to warning signs,
If you want to play the part
First you have to learn your lines.

Forever walking round in circles
And no closer to your goal,
But will you finally get there
When the closing credits roll?

Still higher ever higher
As mediocre will not do
Hoping faith in hope alone
Will somehow pull you through.

A hand to mouth existence
While the days keep sliding by,
There's still no sign of breakthrough
No matter how hard you try.

But dogged perseverance
Drives your weary body on
And only hope alone is left
When everything has gone.

So do not be discouraged
As love will always win,
Just hold on fast and carry on
When you feel like giving in.

WHERE ARE YOU NOW?

Once you were the song I sang
And to your feet my tributes brang,
Echoes of your laughter rang
Another brighter day.

The sun would shine, the sky was blue,
I still believed in dreams come true
You were all I ever knew
Now seems so far away.

A simple word, a sacred prayer
Living life without a care,
Full steam ahead and all set fair
Prepared for come what may.

The timeless day the endless night,
Not knowing why it just seemed right,
From out of darkness into light
Higher powers were at play.

A common purpose, one shared goal,
Two separate halves became one whole,
Combined, entwined both heart and soul
Together making hay.

We had the whole world at our feet
Life was perfect and complete,
Where all our dreams seemed to meet
In magnificent array.

Then summer turned to autumn
And colours fade to grey
Still dreams remain untainted
Of another brighter day.

SOMEWHERE OVER THE RAINBOW

If you say the name
I will name the date,
Not a minute too soon
Nor a moment too late.

Terms of endearment
Or subject to terms,
Nero plays the fiddle
While Rome still burns.

Face to face encounter
Or a stranger in the crowd,
Something on your mind
Or for crying out loud.

A single moment's madness
Just a vision in a dream,
An interlude in paradise
Things aren't always what they seem.

Time to seize the moment
Love will win the day
Do not let the glittering prize
Fade or slip away.

Faint heart nor hesitation
Fair lady ever won,
Just make sure that all is said
When all is said and done.

Fortune favoured bravery
To the victor go the spoils,
A pot of gold at rainbow's end
To show for all your toils.

SEARCH FOR THE HERO INSIDE YOURSELF

Something will only chase you
If you turn and run away,
So face the truth and stand your ground
Because you must embrace the day.

Faith can only overcome if
You confront your greatest fear,
So do not shirk or hide away
When danger's drawing near.

Rise up once more, claim victory,
Show that you won't be beat;
Grab the moment, take the prize
From the jaws of your defeat.

Trials may come to challenge,
The road will not be smooth;
But just a mustard seed of faith
Will make the mountains move.

The darkest hour before the dawn
Heralds the break of day,
If you turn and face the light
The shadows flee away.

The labour pains are worth it,
Just the price you have to pay,
The joy of life for all to see
Is so clearly on display.

The answer is within you,
The potential is in your hands;
For love has got its reasons
Which no reason understands.

TOMORROW BELONGS TO ME

Are you tilting still at windmills?
Are you asking for the moon?
Are you holding on to pipedreams
Or was it over all too soon?

Do you sing your songs of freedom?
Are you just dancing in the dark?
Do you blaze a trail of glory
Or are you searching for a spark?

Where did those days of youth go
And the neverending nights;
The dreams and aspirations
To see your name in lights?

The triumph of former glories
And the shadows they still cast,
When everything was perfect
But was never meant to last.

So celebrate the future
And lay yesterday to rest,
As things worth their weight in gold
Will always stand the test.

You cannot see in front of you
For the sake of looking back
And wherever you are going
Lies somewhere down the track.

In the end you'll finally get there
Though the journey may be long
And the things which do not kill you
Will only make you strong.

KEEP YOUR EYES ON THE PRIZE

I am going back up the mountain
To seek the face of God;
In search of greater wisdom
Where saints of old once trod.

We are all pilgrims on a journey,
Lost souls in need of grace;
Always looking for an answer
Sometime, somewhere, some place.

The road may be less travelled,
The outcome still unknown;
Either sharing life with others
Or marching on alone.

When doubts and indecision
Descend their murky veil,
Just trust in faith in God above
And you'll live to tell the tale.

For every broken promise
And for every stolen dream,
You know one day you'll overcome
However it may seem.

So don't look back in anger,
Lift your heart and raise your eyes;
Fight the good fight and run the race
To claim the glittering prize.

From heaven's halls you have been sent
And to heaven you are bound,
So keep your gaze on heaven
Where your treasures can be found.

PILGRIM'S PROGRESS

Many are called but the chosen are few,
Credit will be given where credit's due.
Destiny beckons but who heeds its call?
The rewards may be great yet the odds are still small.

No fear of failure or shadow of doubt
Only total conviction is what it's about.
Blind to all problems, immune to all pain.
Suffering setbacks but starting again.

Not baulking or flinching at paying the price
Nor counting the cost of each sacrifice.
Determined and focussed, your strength lies within,
You know in yourself that you'll never give in.

The struggle is long and the fight takes its toll
But it's onward and upwards to accomplish your goal.
Though others may falter and fall by the way,
You will still be standing at the end of the day.

You've come this far, there's no turning back,
Complete self-belief is not something you lack.
Full steam ahead to where your fortune lies,
Just one more step to claim the victor's prize.

So walk tall, stand strong for victory is nigh,

Take a glimpse of heaven before the day you die.

Rest's reward will only come when the day is finally done;

The garlands and the trophies when the battle has been won.

We all enter in this life

And we depart it on our own,

But what will you leave behind

As your memorial stone?

GOLD MINING

Buried deep within the soul
Lie precious seams of unmined coal,
Ores of gold and silver too,
Hidden treasures shining through.

Long lost secrets, dreams untold
Like legends once in days of old.
Moths have eaten, grime and dust
Sharpened steel has turned to rust.

But seeds once planted await the rain
The desert soil will bloom again.
For where there's hope there's always life,
The greatest gifts are born of strife.

Necessity is invention's spur
So metamorphosis can occur.
The time has come to shed your skin
And let rebirth and growth begin.

For each there is a season,
A reason and a rhyme;
So shine your light and sparkle,
You know this is your time.

You are an uncut diamond,
A priceless one-off gem;
Immutable and ancient
Which time will not condemn.

So precious and amazing,
A gift beyond compare;
Like rain falling at drought's end
An answer to a prayer.

ONE MORE STEP ON THE ROAD TO JERUSALEM

Out of trial and tribulation
Your faith will sprout and grow;
For every mountain conquered
There must be a valley low.

The path is long and winding
And the journey hard to bear;
But the load can be made lighter
If it's a burden you can share.

You don't have to travel solo,
For you are never on your own;
There is always someone there for you
When you think you are alone.

The choice is pure and simple
As the way ahead is clear;
You can break the chains which hold you
Or you can live your life in fear.

You don't have to suffer heartbreak
Or cry yourself to sleep at night;
So come out from the shadows
And walk into the light.

There is no virtue in complacency
To accept the status quo;
It is better to die trying
Than to never get to know

Of love and life for living
Each day for what it's worth;
To make the most of every moment
As you walk upon this earth.

DREAM ON

Let patience be your watchword,
Let wisdom be your guide,
Place your faith in virtue
Where seeds of hope abide.

Take comfort in small mercies,
Make excellence your aim;
Don't offer lame excuses
Or look to pass the blame.

Do not give in to temptation,
Do not fall prey to sin,
Do not succumb to weakness
Or let your baser nature win.

Select your friends with caution,
Choose your words with care;
Walk tall through all adversity
Despite the scars you bear.

Sing out your songs of freedom,
Release your rebel yell;
When offered opportunity
Be sure to make it tell.

Nurture dreams of grandeur,
Give respect where it is due,
But first you have to have a dream
To have a dream come true.

Consider hope your ally,
Rejoice in all you do;
With grace and due humility
Your faith will see you through.

WHERE EAGLES SOAR

The past is only prologue,
A mere setting of the scene;
From the wisdom of experience
Of what you've done and been.

It is the thrill of the adventure,
A destination not yet reached;
A work that's still in progress
Like a sermon to be preached.

A life now lived in exile,
From your roots across the sea;
Now nurtured you have flourished
To produce a fruitful tree.

The treasures deep within you
Must be cultivated too;
Let the genie out the bottle
To reveal your spirit true.

You have been gifted for a reason,
Your blessings are from on high;
The whole world is your oyster,
Do not let it pass you by.

It is not so much your history
Or merely whence you came;
It is more important where you're going
So make plans and now take aim.

Let faith be your foundation,
You are justified secure;
Both anointed and appointed
With the holy and the pure.

NOW THANK WE ALL OUR GOD

Tonight you took my breath away,
You caused these tears to flow;
You touched the essence of my soul
And you left my heart aglow.

In the presence of the angels,
An encounter with the King;
I feel I am in heaven
When I hear your voices sing.

I will treasure each and every moment
Until the day I die;
It seems that every time I see you
You always make me cry.

Tears of such sweet sorrow
Will help to ease the pain;
Healing hurts of days gone by
Until we meet again.

You are my rivers in the desert,
My rest at journey's end;
A respite from the storms of life,
A true and faithful friend.

I thank God for you dearly
And the world will never know
Just how blessed that I must be
And you how much I owe.

Separated now by distance,
A million miles apart;
But sweet melodies still echo
Forever in my heart.

WHEN

If you believe in love divine
The hope and the glory will be thine.
If you hold on to simple truth
One day you'll live to see the proof.

If you're prepared to fight the fight
You'll overcome and do what's right.
If you refuse to bow to fear
Then carry on and persevere.

If you stand up to raise your voice
For only you can make that choice.
If you defend the widow's claim
And bear the torch of freedom's flame.

If you will hear the orphan's cry
And not decide to walk on by.
If you can feel your brother's pain
To lift him up to rise again.

If you can hope when hope has gone
And find a star to wish upon.
If you delight in serving God
You'll get to walk where saints once trod.

If when all is said and done
And at last the race is run,
You'll finally lay your burden down
And get to wear a golden crown.

For the Lord your God is with you,
No enemy can stand;
Ordained from ages past
You are etched upon His hand.

IF ONLY YOU BELIEVE

You know you can do anything
If you only first believe;
Your gift is your salvation
If you are willing to receive.

There is no mountain high enough,
No goal too hard to reach;
But to overcome all obstacles
You must practise what you preach.

The oak of great ambition
From seeds of faith shall grow;
For nurtured love when watered
Will cause your dreams to flow.

Do not look back in anger
Or dare entertain regret;
The past is merely prologue
Cos you ain't seen nothing yet.

With redemption as your motive
And with virtue as your muse
Let conviction be your yardstick
Just seek destiny to choose.

You were chosen and created
All for such days as these,
The Almighty always listens
When you get down on your knees.

Ring out the bells of liberty,
Do not go back the way you came;
You may be only passing through
But the future knows your name.

REVIVAL FIRE

I dreamt I saw an angel
In a vision from the Lord;
While choirs sang in unison,
The Church of one accord.

I saw the glory coming down
In a dazzling, burning flame;
Every knee bowed before the throne,
Every tongue confessed His name.

Tears of joy from heaven
Were raining down that day;
Floods of generations past
To wipe all pain away.

Reconciliation reached
Between the fathers and the sons;
Mothers, daughters healed once more
Reunited cherished ones.

Oh what celebration scenes
In the Kingdom I did see;
Peace on earth and mercy mild
As the captives were set free.

So send revival rains again
And bring down holy fire;
To delight ourselves in you our God
Our one true heart's desire.

With all eyes fixed on heaven,
Then our heads are bowed in prayer.
We wait in expectation
For the one beyond compare.

GOD'S OWN PEOPLE

You are the prized possession,
The apple of His eye;
Who by your faith's confession
Of the Son he sent to die

Are born into the Kingdom,
For the glory you are bound;
God's praises you shall sing them
And heaven's echo doth resound.

You share a royal birthright,
One blood, one root, one vine;
Each one a beacon's searchlight
By God's grace you burn and shine.

Your commission plainly stated,
You'll be sent to horizons wide;
So that God is celebrated
And his name is glorified.

So fill your heart with gladness,
Let your spirit dance with joy;
There will be no more pain and sadness,
For the yoke He shall destroy.

Precious daughter, precious son,
Priceless jewels, the battle's won;
Go forth by faith you will prevail,
With God with you, you cannot fail.

Protected, safe and sheltered
In the shadow of His wings;
An heir unto the Kingdom,
You serve the King of Kings.

OBEDIENCE NOT SACRIFICE

The Lord is watching over you,
He sees everything you do.
Every act of kindness and every worthy deed,
Each and every effort represents a seed.

So you shall reap a harvest
And much fruit you shall bear;
All that you could ever need
With plenty more to spare.

You sow in righteousness each day,
Now heaven's blessings are on their way.
In the land of the living you shall see
Strongholds fall and captives set free.

You may not understand it
And you need not question why,
Just accept the Lord's bounty
As He shall multiply.

Do not become disheartened
When the wicked prosper in your sight;
Be content with who you are
And continue doing what is right.

Despise not small beginnings,
It is the outcome which will count;
And when it's time for your reward
You'll receive your fair amount.

It is obedience not sacrifice
That will open up the way;
Your God is ever faithful
And He hears you when you pray.

FOR JERUSALEM'S SAKE

For Zion's sake I will not hold my peace,
I will not rest and I shall not cease
Until her righteousness is shining bright
And all men shall see her dazzling light.

Her salvation is a lamp that burns,
Unto her, her remnant returns.
You shall be called by a new name
And you will never be the same.

A holy royal envoy,
An ambassador for Christ;
A vessel now of honour,
A blameless sacrifice.

You shall be a crown of glory
In the hands of the Lord;
The world shall know the story
And you will receive your own reward.

You shall no longer be termed 'Forsaken',
You will be 'Desolate' no more;
Surely you will never be shaken
For God's blessings are in store.

You shall be called Hephzibah
And Beulah is your land;
A royal diadem you are set
In the good Lord's hand.

I have set watchmen on your walls
And they will give you no rest;
Those who reside in heaven's halls
Know that you are truly blessed.

IT JUST AIN'T FUNNY

How much must you love me Lord
When all is said and done?
You gave me life, you showed me love,
You gave your only Son.

You bless me in the morning,
You bless me in the day;
You bless me without warning
In every kind of way.

People are starting to ask questions,
Why is my God so good?
I can only make suggestions,
I would explain it if I could.

But you do not need a reason
To express your love for me;
Both in and out of season
That's just the way it seems to be.

This is only the beginning,
I know there is more to come;
 I am getting used to winning
And the devil's looking glum.

But sometimes Lord it just ain't funny,
It's not just your favour, it ain't just the money.
You simply take my breath away,
More and more Lord, day by day.

Both blessed and highly favoured,
Oh what a mighty God we serve;
All good gifts they come from Him,
So much more than we deserve.

YOU CAN'T BRING ME DOWN

Just when it all seemed over,
And when the cause looked lost;
You called on God Jehovah
And by the power of the cross

You discovered your salvation,
A redemption bought with blood;
You have no explanation
But he came in like a flood.

Angels came to rescue you
In the stillness of the night;
Only God could pull you through
And shine His guiding light.

You were salvaged for a reason
For there is business to be done;
This is your appointed season
To live life in the sun.

You will speak to tribes and nations,
You shall tell your tale abroad
In distant strange locations
And you will work for no reward

Save knowing you are serving God
And doing what is right;
You'll take the paths the saints once trod
And you shall win the fight.

It was the stone that was rejected,
The one that was thrown away;
The one no one would have expected
That is glorified today.

ROOTS

Dig deep to lay foundations
For what is built to last,
Raise preconceived expectations
And consign them to the past.

It is time to stretch your borders,
To enlarge the place of your tent;
You are now under starter's orders
And must be ready to be sent.

Do not doubt your inner voice,
It will not lead you astray;
The way ahead a simple choice
Because you know you cannot stay

Living in mediocre land
When there's so much more to gain;
Your own domain shall soon expand
As you lose your ball and chain.

So sow your seeds unto the winds
For the harvest shall be great;
Pour new wine into new wineskins,
You will not have long to wait.

It is the season of your increase,
It is the year of Jubilee;
Prisoners granted their release
As the captives are set free.

Your plans shall be established sound,
These things will come to pass;
Now build your dreams on solid ground
So they are made to last.

MAKING YOUR MIND UP

Do not tarry, delay or wait,
The price is high but the prize is great.
What have you got to hold onto,
The world outside or Christ in you?

It does not require much thinking,
There really only is one choice;
To desert a ship that's sinking
And to finally raise your voice.

Do not rely on mortal man
To meet your inner needs;
Have faith in the Father's master plan,
He will supply you with good seeds.

Pursue wisdom day and night,
Let it guide your steps and be your light.
Seek the Lord for Godly advice,
Your gain is measured by your sacrifice.

You must choose which way to go,
Will you answer yes or answer no?
Only you can now decide,
To trust in God, He shall provide.

Obey the word upon your heart,
Set yourself and life apart.
Break the shackles, loose the chains,
Prepare to greet the Latter Rains.

You must make the decision,
You know what you must do;
For the only one who really matters
Has every faith in you.

BE OF GOOD COURAGE

The Lord your God will give you grace
To deal with all the trials you face.
You shall have the courage too,
The strength, the faith to pull you thorough.

For you are no longer on your own,
Fruit will flourish where seeds are sown.
Have no fear of mortal man,
What you can't do, well your God can.

Nothing ventured, nothing gained,
Acts of love which are not feigned.
Look around at what you see,
Just turn to Him and be set free.

For you are called to higher planes
Where only truth and love remains.
Your heart is pure, likewise your soul,
Jehovah God is in control.

Rise in might on eagle's wings,
And see what joy that freedom brings.
For you shall know the Father's touch,
You have so little yet want so much.

There is no room for doubting, this is no time to fear;

No haggling or shouting, the way ahead is clear.

For you to shine in glory in the service of the Lord,

To rewrite history's story and to receive your just reward.

Do not let anything come between

Your life today and tomorrow's dream.

Your only wish to do His will,

His holy purpose you shall fulfil.

A LIGHT UNTO THE NATIONS

The Lord hears your petition,
He shall answer to your cry;
God will send aid in your mission.
He will not pass you by.

The angels are preparing
To descend from heaven's halls;
To ease the load you're bearing
And to build Salvations Walls.

This city needs your passion,
This nation yearns for God;
His love and His compassion
Where pilgrim saints once trod.

Your voice shall touch the people,
To heal them from their pain;
The weak, the lost, the feeble
Will know of Christ again.

He will send labourers for the harvest,
There shall be workers in the field;
You will win over even the hardest,
And the coldest heart shall yield.

Have faith, stay strong, you'll overcome;
No longer deaf, no longer dumb.
You've yet to have your finest hour,
You'll walk in grace and move by power.

The Lord your God is on your side;
By faith alone you're justified.
Soon to know of love divine,
Arise in Christ it's time to shine.

EYES THAT SEE

Give me eyes that I might see,
Give me ears that I might hear;
Make me all you've called me to be,
Give me grace that I might draw near.

I want to witness visions,
To dream of things to come;
To speak with such precision,
For thy will to be done.

Grant me courage that I should go
When those around me all say no.
I want to scale the mountain peaks,
You can be found by he who seeks.

I won't settle in my comfort zone,
I'll head off into the great unknown.
I shall not fear temptation's snare,
Or shirk the burden I must bear.

For people are relying
On what I have to say;
The words you put into my mouth
Will drive all doubt away.

Anoint your servant this very hour
With grace and mercy, wisdom's power.
You are the potter, I am the clay,
Mould me in your own sweet way.

I shall follow my conquering King,
And by my deeds His gospel bring.
Lord I give my life to thee,
To become all that I might be.

DELIGHT YOURSELF IN THE LORD

It does not take a prophet
To tell that you'll go far;
Remain on track just serving God,
You're fine the way you are.

Do not become distracted,
Disheartened or misled,
The world will be impacted
By all you've done and said.

Remember well your calling,
You shall be set apart;
When other stars are falling
God will reveal your heart.

He will give you stratagems
And plans to overcome;
Direction, dreams and wisdom
So the battle shall be won.

The Lord knows all your secrets
And the desires which you guard;
You will not have any regrets
Although the road be long and hard.

Concentrate on the job in hand,
Prepare to enter into the land.
Soon to find your hope and joy,
All obstacles He shall destroy.

Tears once shed anoint the ground,
You will now flourish where love is found.
Cherished, treasured and highly esteemed,
You'll become more than you ever dreamed.

SPRINGS OF LIVING WATER

The Lord will use your voice
To bless the nations wide;
Angelic hosts in heaven rejoice
As the spirit in you abides.

There is power in your worship,
The strongholds quake and fall;
Your sacrifice will be worth it
If you answer to the call.

Like a spear in Jehovah's hand
A weapon primed for war;
Your praises echo across the land
And his blessings shall outpour.

Do not maintain your silence,
Proclaim His name on high;
Take the Kingdom by violence
For He is your battle cry.

Sweet melodies like incense
Unto the throne ascend,
Focussed, pure and intense
With joy the heavens rend.

Be reverent and holy,
Both lyrical and fine;
Fresh anointing on your gift
He will pour out the new wine.

So sing your songs of glory,
To the Saviour King of Kings,
You must share the gospel story
Of the Living Water springs.

WE ARE MORE THAN CONQUERORS

Just as Jesus conquered death
He gave us his life, He gave us breath.
He paid the ransom once and for all
And one by one our opponents fall.

For we are overcomers
And in all things shall prevail;
We are above and not below,
The head and not the tail.

We are born to be victorious,
Every battle we will win;
We live a life more abundant
Because we are dead to sin.

No weapon formed against us
Shall prosper in any way;
We condemn every tongue that rises,
Likewise every demon slay.

We have no fear but the fear of God,
And boldly walk where no man's trod.
In times of peace we prepare for war,
We won't back down, one thing's for sure.

All the nations are expectant,
The people wait in awe;
We shall prepare the way for God,
His Spirit to outpour.

Ye soldiers of the cross arise
And put your battle armour on;
It is time that we got serious,
It is time our light was shone.

THE LANGUAGE OF LOVE

Let love be the currency which you use,
How we live is the way we choose.
Forgiving others who do us wrong,
What does not break us will make us strong.

If we stay humble, meek and pure;
Instead of the problem we become the cure.
Loving others with the love of Christ,
Offering ourselves as a sacrifice.

We do not know what good we do
When we embrace our enemies too.
You'll heap coals of fire on their head
If you give them water and give them bread.

What you reap is what you sow,
You must plant seeds to see them grow.
Blessing others make love your aim;
God won't let you be put to shame.

From just one apple an orchard blooms,
A mansion awaits with many rooms.
When your race is finally run
Then you can reflect on all you've done.

Good and faithful servant true,
You shall enter into rest;
But for now the times are urgent,
Go forth and you'll be blessed.

For the God we gladly serve
Is a God of boundless care;
The more love that you have,
The more love you can share.

GOD'S V.I.P.

Anointed and appointed,
Fearfully and wonderfully made;
Equipped, prepared for battle
As foundation stones are laid.

The Lord will do great things through you,
He'll bless your hands in all you do.
When you were formed the mould was broken,
You're the one of whom the prophets have spoken.

You were chosen long before
The day that you were born;
And now the time has finally come
To face your brave new dawn.

Before the birth of civilisation
Your future was assured;
As all the gifts in heaven
Within you now are stored.

It will cause you to walk before Kings
And to receive everything that godliness brings.
Fire will fall upon your tongue
As you climb the ladder rung by rung.

Nations need your counsel,
Kingdoms your wisdom seek;
You shall inherit all the earth
If you stay humble and meek.

So rise up now on eagle's wings
The gospel to proclaim;
On honour God in all you do,
He shall make great your name.

TREASURE IN HEAVEN

You have to make a choice now
As to which way you will go;
Further into the worldly maze
Or will you just say no?

You need to get your values straight,
Who do you want to serve?
Do you still seek the praise of men
And glory here on earth?

You must not get distracted
By all the flattering acclaim;
You should seek your satisfaction
From the one who gave you your name.

The world will offer you cheap trinkets
And mere baubles you can hold;
But you would do well to remember
That all that glitters is not gold.

You can not satisfy two masters,
There can't be room for any doubt;
If you are true God will accept you,
If you are lukewarm spit you out.

He sees what is inside your heart
And He knows your real desire;
But you must decide just what you want
And to what you now aspire.

You can choose to follow Jesus
And so live your life by grace;
Or trust your baser instincts
And you will vanish without trace.

MOVING TO HIGHER GROUND

It is the season of revival,
The Kingdom's coming down;
It is a fight for our survival
And the right to wear the crown.

The Lord is our provider,
He will meet our every need;
Like the ravens for Elijah,
He will give to us the seed.

So that we can plant a vineyard
And reap a harvest of the lost;
But first we must look inward
And be prepared to pay the cost.

We'll give up our lives that we might live,
And when Jesus arrives, our testimony give.
If you leave your comfort zone behind
Fresh new horizons you will find.

Sacrifice the life you know,
Pack your bags it's time to go.
What do you think you have to lose?
The moment of truth, it's time to choose.

Better days are on their way,
All you need to do is pray.
Love is your banner, justice your cause;
Heavy sky of manna around you softly falls.

You are blessed and highly favoured,
You are the apple of His eye;
With great riches to be savoured
As His name you glorify.

DO THE RIGHT THING

Camera, lights and action,
The stage will soon be set;
There shall be no distraction,
All your deadlines will be met.

You serve the Master humbly
And He shall lift you on high;
You are young, keen, bright and hungry
And there is no reason why

All your dreams can't be achieved
If you use the gift which you've received
To honour God and share His love,
He'll pour out blessings from above.

You can't afford to compromise,
Despite the jibes, the hurt, the lies.
Identify your heart's desire,
Delight in Him and light a fire.

A flame to burn both night and day
Let wisdom guide you as you pray.
There is a calling on your life
Sharper than the sharpest knife.

You can change a generation
If you obey what God ordains;
You can slay giants and take Kingdoms
Break the shackles and loose chains.

You can walk out into destiny
And rise up to higher ground;
Or remain inside your dungeon
Left silenced, weak and bound.

RIVERS IN THE DESERT

Where once was only darkness,
Now you shall bring the light;
As soon the break of dawn
Will end the longest night

With wisdom for the vacant
And direction for the lost;
Redeemed, ordained, forgiven,
You are a child of Calvary's cross.

A friend unto the lonely,
A champion of the poor;
The Lord is going to bless you
And then He'll bless you more.

For you have been given a commission,
A dream, a plan, a goal;
In this season of refreshing
He shall revive your soul.

Closer now than ever before,
You've been through much, there's more in store.
Guard your lips, your counsel keep,
Allow the idle to soundly sleep.

It is time for getting serious,
The talking has to cease;
Your treasures housed in heaven
He is shortly to release.

From their slumber God shall rouse,
Convict their hearts, renew their vows
Walk upright with conscience clear,
The Lord Jehovah is drawing near.

HONOUR THE LORD

I know now what I've got to do;
Whatever it takes to honour you.
I shall sow a seed that I might reap
A yield enough to feed your sheep.

I can hear their distant voices,
My heart echoes their lament,
And as heaven rejoices
I will go where I am sent.

I praise my heavenly Father
For all I have received,
But this is just a starter
For which I have believed.

I pray for your direction
For the journey up ahead;
For divine grace and protection
Now I have done what you have said.

I thank you Lord my eternal light
In days of trial and darkest night.
But now the dawn is soon to break,
The flame revived, my soul awake.

No more to wait and just look on,

Immune to pain when things were wrong.

What will be your legacy,

Abundant fruit or barren tree?

A light unto the nations,

A gift to all who hear;

The hour of refreshing

Is slowly drawing near.

WAKE UP CALL

For each there is a reason,
A season and a time;
We must survive the trials of life
If we are to reach our prime.

Salvation with a purpose
To justify the cross;
To toil and strive for victory
When all else counts as loss.

You can only serve one master,
There are choices to be made;
If you are dancing with the devil
Then the piper must be paid.

You cannot feign indifference,
Ignorance is no defence
And a pocketful of alibis
Are not making any sense.

You will not pass this way again,
It is time to play for real.
Moths will eat and rust devour
What the locusts do not steal.

What will it take to rouse you
From the slumber of your sleep?
You may well be sowing seeds today
Which tomorrow you must reap.

These things you see are temporary,
They all shall pass away;
But you will have to face your maker
And explain on Judgement Day.

About the Author

Ian Field was born in Croydon in 1963. From early on, his life taught him that miracles are both possible and likely – all we need is the belief through which to see them.

For many years Ian has expressed his faith through poetry. In this collection we find words to console, inspire, explain and, above all, remind us that life is about following the true and faithful path, ever mindful that our destinies are unfolding in the eternal light and love of the Lord.

Lightning Source UK Ltd.
Milton Keynes UK
178043UK00001B/6/P